Who Feels Scared?

Written by Sue Graves

Illustrated by
Desideria Guicciardini

W

FRANKLIN WATTS
LONDON • SYDNEY

Last night, Robin and Ravi
stayed at Jack's house.
They were very
excited!

In Jack's bedroom, they heard a noise.
Robin thought it was a **lion.**
Ravi thought it was a **tiger.**
They were so scared they hid!

But Jack wasn't **scared at all.**

Jack said it wasn't a lion or a tiger.
He said it was Pip, the dog.
And Pip **wasn't scary at all!**

Then they all heard a *really* scary noise.
It was coming from Jack's cupboard.
They thought it was a monster.

They thought it was a **huge** monster.
They got so scared, they yelled.

Jack's sister, Ellie, came in.
They told her about the
monster in the cupboard.
But Ellie wasn't scared.

She looked in the cupboard.
It wasn't a monster.
It was Jack's toy robot.
And that **wasn't scary at all.**

Ellie said she got scared
sometimes. She said
she was scared of
flying!

Robin, Ravi and Jack weren't scared of flying.

They thought flying was fun.

Ellie thought planes were
big and noisy.

But she liked going on holiday!

So she always played music
when she had to fly.

Then flying wasn't scary at all.

Ellie said Pip got scared sometimes, too. She said Pip was scared of **fireworks.**

But Robin, Ravi and Jack weren't scared of fireworks.

They thought fireworks **were fun.**

Pip didn't like fireworks that flashed and banged. He thought they were **noisy and scary.**

So Jack always switched on the TV for
Pip. And Ellie played ball with him.
Then the fireworks...

...weren't scary **at all!**

Jack's dad came in.
He said it was time for bed.
He read everyone a story.

But it was a **very** **scary** **Story.**
And **everyone** yelled and hid!

Then they remembered it was only a story! Jack's dad said that everyone gets scared sometimes!

Can you tell the story of Tom's first night away from home, staying at his gran's house?

How do you think Tom felt when he left his mum and dad? How did he feel when he went to bed?

A note about sharing this book

The *Our Emotions and Behaviour* series has been developed to provide a starting point for further discussion on children's feelings and behaviour, both in relation to themselves and to other people.

Who Feels Scared?
This story explores in a reassuring way some of the typical fears that children, adults and even animals experience. It also points out that different things frighten different people and that not everyone is afraid of the same things.

The book aims to encourage children to have a developing awareness of their own needs, views and feelings, and to be sensitive to the needs, views and feelings of others.

Storyboard puzzle
The wordless storyboard on pages 26 and 27 provides an opportunity for speaking and listening. Children are encouraged to tell the story illustrated in the panels: Tom is nervous about his first night staying away from home at his gran's house. Soon he enjoys joining in a game with his gran. Perhaps he is reassured by his teddy? By the end of the story, he is happily saying goodnight.

How to use the book
The book is designed for adults to share with either an individual child, or a group of children, and as a starting point for discussion.

The book also provides visual support and repeated words and phrases to build confidence in children who are starting to read on their own.

Before reading the story
Choose a time to read when you and the children are relaxed and have time to share the story.

Spend time looking at the illustrations and talk about what the book may be about before reading it together.

After reading, talk about the book with the children:

- What was it about? Have the children stayed the night with friends? How did they feel? Did they feel afraid about sleeping in a strange room? What did they do to help them feel less scared? Did they, for example, find a night-light made them feel better? Or did a favourite toy, such as a teddy, make them feel safer?

  Encourage the children to talk about their experiences.

- Extend this discussion by talking about other things that make the children feel afraid. Who do they tell if they feel afraid? Would they tell a friend or an adult they know and trust?

- Now talk about the things that might scare adults. Some may, like Ellie, be nervous of flying or perhaps scared of things such as spiders...or mice! Siblings in their families may have other fears ranging from a fear of thunder and lightning to going up to senior school.

  Point out that different things scare different people.

- Take the opportunity to talk about the things that frighten animals, especially loud noises such as those from fireworks.

  Talk about how to help animals at such times.

- Look at the end of the story again. All the characters were afraid of the scary story told by Dad. Talk about the things that scare the children and how they can overcome their fears.

- Look at the storyboard puzzle. Can the children talk about Tom's first night away from home at his gran's house? Can they see anything in the pictures that made Tom feel better when he was nervous?

  What else can they think of that can help them feel more confident?

  Suggest drawing a picture of what makes them feel better when they are afraid.

This edition 2014
Franklin Watts
338 Euston Road
London
NW1 3BH

Franklin Watts Australia
Level 17/207 Kent Street
Sydney
NSW 2000

A CIP catalogue record for this book is available
from the British Library.

ISBN 978 1 4451 2989 1 (paperback)
ISBN 978 1 4451 2130 7 (library ebook)

Editors: Adrian Cole and Jackie Hamley
Designers: Jonathan Hair and Peter Scoulding

Printed in China

Franklin Watts is a division of
Hachette Children's Books,
an Hachette UK company.
www.hachette.co.uk